# CERTAINTY
# OF
# BIBLE PROPHECY

# CERTAINTY OF BIBLE PROPHECY

## Dr. Robert Lindsted

**Hearthstone Publishing Ltd.**

P.O. Box 815·Oklahoma City, Ok 73101

*A Division Of*
**Southwest Radio Church Of The Air**

All scripture references are from the King James Version unless otherwise stated.

**The Certainty Of Bible Prophecy**
First Edition, 1991
Copyright © by **Hearthstone Publishing, Ltd.**

*Printed in the United States of America*

Published by:
**Hearthstone Publishing, Ltd.**
P.O. Box 815
Oklahoma City, OK 73101

**ISBN 1-879366-07-X**

# Contents

# *Saddam Hussein, The Persian Gulf, And The End Times*

Whenever we look at current events in light of Bible prophecy, there are always a number of people that become very nervous, and some become quite excited. I am reminded of the story of a young girl who left home to go to college. She decided that she would take some pictures of the campus and send them home to mom and dad. As she went around the campus, she eventually came to the fountain. She accidentally dropped her camera, and it settled to the bottom of the fountain. About that time, her history professor came walking down the sidewalk. The young girl, not sure what to do about her camera, came up to the professor and said, "Sir, I don't know if you remember me or not, but I'm a freshman in your history class." "Well," he said, "what has that got to do with me?" She answered, "Well, I was wondering if you could help me get my camera. You see, I was taking pictures, and I dropped it into the fountain." To this he responded, "I can't believe that you'd ask me. I'm about fifty years old, and this is the best suit I own. It seems like an attractive girl like you could find some young man that would be willing to . . ." At this point the girl interrupted, "Oh, I know I could find some young man to do it, but already from sitting through your lectures I know that

1

you can go down deeper, stay under longer, and come up drier than anyone I know."

Maybe that has always been how you react to discussions of current events in light of Bible prophecy. But, right now, we are witnessing incredible events taking place in our world. As we witness history being made, we need to remember that history is actually the fulfillment of Bible prophecy.

We can go all the way back to the Old Testament books of Daniel, Jeremiah, and Isaiah and find the prophecy of events that are taking place right now in the Persian Gulf — events recorded hundrds of years ago. Everything we're seeing is a part of God's Word being fulfilled exactly as it was recorded hundreds of years ago.

As we look at the fourth chapter of the book of Daniel, remember that it deals with King Nebuchadnezzar, the great king of Babylon of yesteryear. Also remember that today Babylon is known as Iraq, and when we talk of the king of Iraq, we're talking about Saddam Hussein.

Daniel 4:1-4,10-15,20-22 reads:

*"Nebuchadnezzar the king, unto all the people, nations, languages, that dwell in all the earth; Peace be multiplied unto you. I thought it good to shew the signs and wonders that the high God hath wrought toward me. How great are his signs! and how mighty are his wonders! his kingdom is an everlasting kingdom, and his dominion is from generation to generation. I, Nebuchadnezzar, was at rest in mine house, and flourishing in my palace . . . Thus were the visions of mine head in my bed; I saw, and behold*

*a tree in the midst of the earth, and the height of it was great. The tree grew, and was strong, and its height reached unto heaven, and the sight it to the end of all the earth. Its leaves were fair, and its fruit much, and in it was food for all the beasts of the field, they had shadow under it, the fowls of the heavens dwelt in its branches, and all flesh was fed from it. I saw in the visions of my head upon my bed, and, behold, a watcher and a holy one came down from heaven; He cried aloud, and said thus, Hew down the tree, cut off its branches, shake off its leaves, scatter its fruit: let the beasts get away from under it, and the fowls from its branches; Nevertheless leave the stump of his roots in the earth, even with the band of iron and bronze, in the tender grass of the fields; and let him be wet with the dew from heaven, and let his portion be with the beasts in the grass of the earth . . . The tree that thou sawest, which grew, and was strong, whose height reached unto the heaven, and the sight of it to all the earth; whose leaves were fair, and the fruit much, and in it was food for all; under which the beasts of the field dwelt, and upon whose branches the fowls of the heaven had their habitation: It is thou, O king, that art grown and become strong; for thy greatness is grown, and reached into heaven, and thy dominion is to the end of earth."*

In verses twenty-four through twenty-six it says that because of his pride, he was to be lifted up, he would be cut off, and the tree would be cut down.

We next read Daniel 4:28-34, which says:

*"All this came upon the king Nebuchadnezzar. At the end of twelve months he walked in the palace of his kingdom. The king spoke and said, Is not this great Babylon, that I have built for the house of the kingdom by the might of my power, and for the honour of my majesty? While the word was in the king's mouth, there fell a voice from heaven, saying, O king Nebuchadnezzar, to thee it is spoken; The kingdom is departed from thee. And they shall drive thee from men, and thy dwelling shall be with the beasts of the field: they shall make thee eat grass as oxen, and seven times* [that's seven years] *shall pass over thee, until thou know that the most High ruleth in the kingdom of men, and giveth it to whomsoever he will. The same hour was the thing fulfilled upon Nebuchadnezzar: and he was driven from men, and did eat grass as oxen, and his body was wet with the dew of heaven, till his hairs were grown like eagles' feathers, and his nails like birds' claws. And at the end of the days* [the seven years] *I Nebuchadnezzar lifted up mine eyes unto heaven, mine understanding returned unto me, and I blessed the most High, and I praised and honoured him who liveth for ever, whose dominion is an everlasting dominion, and his kingdom is from generation to generation."*

What we find in Daniel 4 is an ancient king of Babylon who thought that he was a world controller and a world leader. Because of this, God gave him a dream saying that because of his pride, because of his arrogance, God would cut down Babylon for seven years. Secular history verifies exactly the story we read.

History records that Nebuchadnezzar had a mental breakdown and for those seven years, literally, he made his home in the palace yard. His hair was not cut, his fingernails were not trimmed, and as a result he looked more like an animal than he did a man. Then after the seven years, there was a remarkable recovery. According to Daniel 4, at the end of Nebuchadnezzar's life he actually came to Christ for he came to understand the plan of God.

As we look in the book of Daniel at the great world power called Babylon with its great king who was a ruthless leader, we should remember that the power Nebuchadnezzar had is actually the power that the Antichrist someday will have over the whole world. The palace and the kingdom of Babylon are today the palace and the kingdom of Iraq. Even the secular press knows this to be true.

When was the last time you saw *Time* or *U.S. News and World Report* begin their articles quoting from the book of Daniel? One particular article from *Time* magazine, August 13, 1990, is entitled "Master Of His Universe." It begins this way: *"The book of Daniel, chapter 4 verse 33, 'Nebuchadnezzar was driven from men, and he ate grass like oxen.' "* The article goes on:

*"What kind of a man would cold-bloodedly*

*gobble up a neighboring country? What kind of a man would try to assassinate a prime minister? What kind of man gasses undefended villages or executes his closest colleagues? What kind of a man is Iraq's president for life Saddam Hussein?"*

*Time* goes on to say that Hussein sees himself as Nebuchadnezzar, *Time* claiming that recently Hussein had his picture taken in a replica of a war chariot of Nebuchadnezzar's day because he lives and sleeps and thinks of himself as Nebuchadnezzar. The reason this makes him so dangerous, continues the article, is because, according to the book of Daniel, Nebuchadnezzar made his name in history by destroying Jerusalem in 587 B.C. The article goes on to state that because Nebuchadnezzar took Syria, Lebanon, and Israel, Hussein's desire is to also take Syria, Lebanon, and Israel.

Another article in the same issue of *Time*, on page 16, begins: *"Iraq's Power Grab. Not since the brilliant military leader Nebuchadnezzar ruled the Babylon Empire more than 2,000 years ago has Baghdad exercised such sway."* Then it goes on to show the parallel between Nebuchadnezzar in ancient Babylon and Hussein in modern-day Iraq.

Could it really be that what we have is a person who thinks he is living a dream? The dream of Nebuchadnezzar was a nightmare for him, and Hussein's dream may be a nightmare for him and the world.

As I point out articles from the *New York Times* and *Time* magazine, I want to remind you that such newspapers and magazines are all the secular press. They are written by reporters, not Bible teachers or preachers. Here is what they point out in the *New York Times*, August 13, 1990, page A14:

> *"As for the isolated Hussein, he might ponder the fate of those Babylonian kings with whom he likens himself. Nebuchadnezzar, the book of Daniel tells us, was once so powerful that all the peoples, nations, languages trembled in fear before him. But as pride betrayed him, they disposed of his kingly throne, and his glory was taken from him. This lesson was not learned. Belshazzar, his successor, also grew dangerously intoxicated with his own might and importance. One day the fingers of a man's hand appeared and inscribed on the palace wall. It announced the abrupt end of his reign. Is the handwriting already on Iraq's walls?"*

Isn't it amazing that the *New York Times* would draw a parallel between the old king of Babylon, Nebuchadnezzar and the modern king of Iraq, Hussein?

An article from the *Milwaukee Journal*, on August 12, 1990, by the editorialist Cal Thomas is entitled "The Man Who Would Be Nebuchadnezzar." In this article, Cal Thomas displays the thinking of Hussein. In history, the Nebuchadnezzar of Daniel 4 is called "Nebuchadnezzar II." When Hussein writes about himself, he calls himself "Nebuchadnezzar III." He claims that his whole desire is to someday conquer the same territory as Nebuchadnezzar II.

The *Gospel Truth*, published by the Southwest

Radio Church, documents in their August 1990 edition the fact that Saddam Hussein thinks of himself as a reincarnation of Nebuchadnezzar. He is intent on restoring the glory of Babylon, but he is also intent on destroying Israel and the other nations just as his hero did. Could it be that we are watching a man trying to re-enact history? If that's true, maybe it would do us well to look at some of the prophecies in the Bible concerning Babylon.

There was an interesting article in the *Dispatch Jerusalem Post*, during the first quarter of 1990, long before the trouble broke out in Kuwait. It was titled "Ancient Wonders To Be Restored." The dateline was Babylon. It states:

> *"Trying to recover its Babylonian heritage, Iraq is offering a reward to anyone who can restore the marvel of one of the world's seven ancient wonders. President Hussein can bring the legendary hanging gardens of Babylon back to life."*

Then the article goes on to point out that Hussein's idea is to make Babylon into a great tourist attraction. His ultimate plan calls for hotels, restaurants, playgrounds, theaters, and cinemas, many designed in the ancient Babylonian architectural style.

Another revealing article is from the *New York Times International Journal*, April 19, 1989. This was over a year before the invasion into Kuwait. It points out:

> *"When King Nebuchadnezzar ran things around Babylon 2,500 years ago, he left clear instructions*

*for future kings of Babylon. These instructions are finally being carried out. Every brick in the palace that is being reconstructed has inscribed on it, 'Nebuchadnezzar, King of Babylon, from sea to sea.' And, before Hussein will let them rebuild this very palace, using the very bricks of his hero Nebuchadnezzar the second, he has each of them inscribed with his own name, Hussein, or Nebuchadnezzar III."*

It is marvelous how God is allowing us to see a great literal fulfillment of exactly what the Bible warns of hundreds of years ago.

An article from the *Milwaukee Journal*, entitled "History, Is It Being Repeated?" says:

*"Hussein is making his claim for power through military might. What he really wants is not just oil or power; he wants the destruction of Israel."*

On the *Tonight* program, they interviewed one of the foreign ministers of Iraq. He said:

*"We would be willing to give back Kuwait if Israel would be willing to give back the West Bank."*

All of a sudden, without Israel even having been mentioned, they begin to negotiate for the West Bank. It is becoming clear to just about everyone that Hussein's plan has more to do with the Arabs and the Jews than it does with oil. Hussein is going to use everything he can to bring about his dream. And that dream is larger than Kuwait, and it's larger than the Arab kingdom. It also includes the land of Israel.

The *Economist*, August 25, 1990, calls Hussein "The Man With No Illusions." It states that ever since his invasion of Iran in 1980, the Iraqi president has made it clear that he will use any means possible, any means at his disposal, to the extent of his Iraqi power to get what he wants. His ambitions are vast — to lead the Arabs to defy the West and to destroy Israel. How amazing that people in the secular press see exactly the plan that is going on!

In terms of monetary operations, there's no question why Hussein did what he did to Kuwait. He owes Kuwait billions of dollars. The estimate is $15 billion. By invading them, the debt was "forgiven." He seized close to $100 billion in foreign assets and another $50 billion in Kuwait assets. So, in terms of money, it was a great move by Hussein. But I don't believe that he's finished. He has a zeal for power just as Nebuchadnezzar had.

As we look at what the Bible has to say about the future of Babylon [Iraq], we need to look at the book of Jeremiah. Jeremiah 50 and 51 deal specifically with Babylon. It begins, *"The word that the Lord spake against Babylon. . . ."* This will reveal a judgment that God's Word will give against Babylon. Now, the easy thing to say is, "Wasn't this fulfilled a long time ago? How do we know that a passage like this applies to today?" That's a good and fair question which has a good answer.

In order to understand these two chapters, we need to look at Jeremiah 51:62:

*"Then shalt thou say, O Lord, thou hast spoken*

*against this place* [Babylon], *to cut it off, that none shall remain in it. Neither man nor beast, but that it shall be desolate for ever."*

If these words were fulfilled literally, how could there be people in the last decade rebuilding ancient Babylon? The *Jerusalem Dispatch*, the *New York Times*, and other magazines document that Hussein, over the last ten years has been rebuilding the ancient palace of Babylon. It has become a tourist attraction. Art concerts and music concerts have been held there, and yet, the Bible said it would be desolate forever.

I propose that the Bible is one hundred percent accurate in its prophecies. But, may I also suggest this simply means that the final destruction of Babylon has not yet been completed. In Isaiah 21:9 it says, *"Babylon is fallen, is fallen."* In other words, Babylon is predicted to fall twice. There was one ancient fall, under the Medes and Persians, and there will be another fall. It might occur when there is a king of Iraq, or of Babylon, who sees himself with pride, lifted up, hoping to take a spoil, and particularly desiring to take Israel. It says in verse eight that when they come against Babylon that there will be a multitude of nations, not just two, but a whole multitude. There will be a people held hostage, a mingled people from many nations. In verse thirty-seven, it says that they will come, and there will be a mixed people, or a multitude of people from all nations that will be held in Iraq, or Babylon. Is this not the very drama that we have been watching?

Let's continue the documentation of these events with a number of articles from the secular press.

*Newsweek*, August 13, 1990, on page 21 refers to the events in an article entitled "Target Jerusalem." Less than three weeks after the invasion took place, even *Newsweek* said:

> *"The real match is not Kuwait and Iraq; it's not Saudi Arabia and the oil. The real match is between Israel and Iraq."*

Of great interest is an article in *Time* magazine, April 16, 1990. On page 30, it says, "Stumbling Toward Armageddon?" Now, remember that this was printed about five months before the invasion took place and already Saddam Hussein was saying, "I swear to God we will let our fire eat half of Israel if it tries to wage anything against Iraq." So far Israel hasn't launched an attack against anybody.

The Bible says that there will come a day when the Arab nations will be divided. The Bible says that there will be a day when the Egyptian people will drown in the desert. The Bible says that there will be a day when the land of Edom and Moab [the land of Jordan], with its principal city of Amman, will become the territory of Israel. These will all take place at a day when Iraq is rendered desolate.

I really believe that as we look at this situation, we are looking at a page right out of God's Word. The warning to the world from the Bible is that this particular period of time would be in the last days. The very next thing that could take place, according to the Bible, is that there will be a catching out of those who have accepted Christ as their personal Savior. It's called the rapture of the church. Each person who has acknowledged before God that he is a sinner, whether Jew or Gentile, rich or poor, young or old, will be taken out of this world to meet Christ in the clouds. The Bible says that every person who has acknowledged that they are sinners and have come to Jesus Christ's death on the cross for the payment of their sin, will meet Christ in the clouds when He comes back the second time. I believe that is the very next event that the Bible promises.

The Bible also promises a time called the Tribulation. It will begin in a very remarkable way. The Bible says that Israel, according to Daniel 9:27, will actually sign a peace treaty with the Antichrist. Because the Jews rejected Jesus Christ, the real Prince of Peace, they will be deceived by a false man of peace, a false Christ. And that false Christ will actually cause Israel to sign a peace treaty.

It says in Ezekiel 38 that this will occur at a time when Germany is united. It says in Ezekiel 36 that it will occur when Israel is back in its original land. It will be a time when the deserts are blooming in Israel. What a thrill to go to Israel and to drive along a road and see farms on both sides! Some of those farms are growing three and four, some seven crops a year. Those same roads that would have led you through the desert five years ago, today lead you through lush farmland exactly as the Bible predicted.

The Bible says that there would be cities destroyed but then rebuilt in the last days. Five of them exist today. The Bible says that you will know the last days because Israel, the whipping post for other nations for hundreds of years, will have a great army. The Bible says you'll know because Israel, like a valley of dry bones, will be raised up and be a nation again.

The Bible goes a step further. It says that in the last days Russia will actually be falling; it will be stumbling. Think about Russia's condition today. But don't be fooled. I think that Russia is still dangerous. Like a wounded bear, Russia may be more dangerous than before its current situation. In the last days, Israel will sign a peace treaty with the Antichrist, not knowing he is the Antichrist but thinking he is the Messiah. Israel will lay down its weapons, and when this happens, Russia will invade out of the north. With Russia will be other countries — Iran, a united Germany, Turkey, Ethiopia, and Libya.

The Bible says that Russia will want money and need food when it makes its invasion. Look around at Russia today. It is a country desperate for food. It is a country desperate for money.

But back to Israel. Why would Israel sign a treaty with anyone, even the Antichrist? Why would Israel sign a treaty with anyone while the danger in the Middle East still exists? I don't believe Israel will sign a peace treaty with anyone until Hussein has been disarmed, and I don't think Hussein will ever be disarmed peacefully. I believe that if it was possible to disarm Hussein, our president would have given instructions to send another hundred thousand men to the Persian Gulf.

Among the chemicals mentioned in Hussein's germ warfare arsenal is one that has been used before. Forty some years ago this chemical was tried by our own forces. The name of the chemical is anthrax. The article says that when anthrax is released on a piece of ground, it is a considerable period of time before anything — people, plants, or animals — can live there. This is exactly the chemical with which Saddam Hussein threatens Israel. He says that if the wind conditions are correct, they could, by bombing one spot, wipe out ninety-eight percent of the population of Israel in a three to five day period.

Probably the earliest description of anthrax is found in the book of Exodus. We think that the fifth plague of Egypt was none other than anthrax. Our own government, along with England, released anthrax on a small island off the Scotland coast over forty years ago. To this day, no man, animal, or plant life can exist there.

The things that we are reading from the secular press simply show that what is going on is exactly what the Bible mentions. Jeremiah 50:9 says:

*"For, lo, I will raise and cause to come up against Babylon an assembly of great nations from the north country: and they shall set themselves in an array against her. . . ."*

In other words, this predicts an embargo. In an unprecedented move, the United Nations, all the nations of the world, brought sanctions against Hussein. Jeremiah says there will be an assembly, a multitude of great nations, and they will bring an embargo against Babylon. Then, notice Jeremiah 50:19:

*"This will come to pass when I will bring Israel again to his habitation, and he shall feed on Carmel and Bashan. . . ."*

Bashan is the area of the Golan Heights. Do you

realize that the Bible said that when these events take place it will be when Israel is back in its land? Bashan, or the Golan Heights, was not restored to Israel until the 1973 war. Next, we read verse 20:

> *"In those days* [at the very time when Israel comes back to the land, when they have the Golan Heights] *and in that time, saith the Lord, the iniquity of Israel shall be sought for, and there shall be none; and the sins of Judah, and they shall not be found: for I will pardon them whom I reserve."*

He says He will forgive them for their trespasses, because there will be an enemy coming against them in an unfair way. Verse 22 says:

> *"The sound of the battle is at hand, and it will be a great destruction."*

One translation says this destruction of Babylon will be a noisy one, a fierce battle. It also says in verse 26:

> *"Come against* [Babylon] *from the utmost border, open her storehouses: cast her up as heaps, destroy her utterly: let nothing of her be left."*

There will be total destruction.

As you look at these things, remember they were not fulfilled the very first time Babylon was destroyed. Babylon remained, after the Medes and Persians conquered it in 500 B.C., a major city for several hundred years. When the Meddes and Persians took over Babylon, even though they conquered the kingdom, they did not destroy the palaces. For the next two hundred years, every world power that ruled the world ruled from the palace in Babylon. Even Alexander the Great, when he conquered the world, even though his home was in Greece, set up his headquarters in Babylon. That was how marvelous that palace was. It was one of the ancient wonders of the world. Alexander the Great actually died in Babylon, in Iraq. Even, several hundred years after he was destroyed and his kingdom split up, the city of Babylon still existed.

Babylon was destroyed the first time when it was buried under a hundred feet of sand as the Euphrates River changed its course. The second time will be different. Jeremiah 50:29-32 says that the weapons used will be great. There will be many weapons, many nations. It says in verse thirty that all the young men shall fall on the street. In other words, I believe that this will be such an incredible war that hundreds of thousands of young men's lives will be destroyed because of one man's greedy, prideful desire to rule as Nebuchadnezzar and all the territories associated with him.

It says in Jeremiah 50:32:

*"And the most proud shall stumble and fall, and none shall raise him up: and I will kindle a fire in his cities, and it shall devour all round about him."*

In other words, all the area around him will be

destroyed. Look at Jeremiah 50:40:

*"As God overthrew Sodom and Gomorrah and the neighbouring cities, saith the Lord; so shall no man abide there, neither shall any son of man dwell in her."*

Doesn't that sound like no life will continue there? That's why I believe we are on the very brink of seeing this very thing fulfilled. For Sodom and Gomorrah were not destroyed with sand, but with fire and with brimstone.

Very soon Israel will sign a treaty with the Antichrist. Instead of a peaceful time for Israel, it will be a time of doom that the Bible predicted. But I believe as we look at this coming it should be a stern warning to every one of us that we are living in the last days. For those who have accepted Christ as Lord and Savior, I believe that we are coming to a time when we ought to be looking for Christ to come.

Today we have people who are religious, people who think they are on the way to Heaven because they're good or because they attend church. But the Bible is clear that unless a person has received by faith the finished work of Jesus Christ on the cross, His death and His resurrection, and Christ's blood, shed on the cross, there is no hope of salvation. And if Christ were to come, those people that are religious would be left on the earth to go through the time of tribulation. That time of tribualtion described in the book of Revelation is even worse than what we've read in the book of Jeremiah. Let's look at Jeremiah 50:41:

*"Behold, a people shall come from the north,*

*and a great nation, and many kings shall be raised up from the borders of the earth."*

In other words, there will be one nation that will take the lead and bring other countries against Hussein to try to stop him. But he will be cruel and have no mercy and will have to be destroyed. Jeremiah 50:45 gives quite a statement at the end of the verse:

*". . . Surely the least of the flock shall draw them out."*

The Bible says a small nation. Kuwait is a small nation. As you look at a map that shows the Middle East, it is interesting to see how small Kuwait is compared to Saudi Arabia, to Iraq, and to the other nations. The Bible says that a small nation will draw them out and because of that He will make their habitation desolate. As Iraq tries to destroy Israel, God will allow Iraq to be destroyed. *"At the noise of the taking of Babylon the earth is moved, and the cry is heard among the nations."* This will be a world event. It won't be just the fighting of a few Arab tribes but a world event in which all the world will be moved. When nuclear weapons go off, and when chemical weapons go off, such as are being armed right now, I believe all the earth will be moved.

Jeremiah 51:3 says that her young men will not be spared for they will be destroyed, all of them. Then we read in Jeremiah 51:8:

*"Babylon is suddenly fallen and destroyed. Wail over her because her destruction will be great."*

Time and time again Jeremiah mentions that Israel will take over the land of the destruction of Iraq. Then we come to verse 62:

*"Then saith the Lord, thou hast spoken against this place* [Babylon], *to cut it off, that none should remain in it, neither man nor beast, but that it should be desolate forever."*

Because of chemicals and maybe nuclear warfare, the city of Babylon could be desolate forever.

Passages in Isaiah refer to the same time at which we've been looking — the last days, the latter times. In Isaiah 10:20-21, it confirms that this will take place in a day when the remnant of Israel has escaped, and gone back to live in the land of Israel. Isaiah 11:11 says that this will take place when Israel has been united as one nation again. Israel was two nations, Judah and Israel, but in 1948 they came back as a united nation. Isaiah says that Israel will be united at the time of Babylon's judgment.

Isaiah also mentions that there will be a split among all the Arab nations. For the first time in a long time, we see a split among these nations. Verse fourteen says that there will be the destruction of the land of Edom and Moab, and the children of Ammon shall obey Israel. That has never been fulfilled. But if there is a battle between Israel and Iraq, the fighting could well take place in Jordan. Recently, Queen Nor came on television and said, "My people, and my children may be victims of a war between Iraq and Israel." She begged this country for mercy in going against the Iraqis because of the position of her country.

In Isaiah 13:5-6;9-10 we read of the army that will come against Babylon:

*"They come from a far country, from the end of the heaven, even the Lord, and the weapons of his indignation, to destroy the whole land. Wail, for the day of the Lord is at hand; it shall come as a destruction from the Almighty . . . Behold, the day of the Lord cometh, cruel both with wrath and fierce anger, to lay the land desolate: and he shall destroy the sinners thereof out of it. For the stars of heaven and the constellations thereof shall not give their light: the sun shall be darkened in his going forth, and the moon shall not cause her light to shine."*

Those are all end time events that have not yet happened. I really believe that the Bible says that these things are just around the corner.

Then in Isaiah 21 it says there is going to be a great destruction, and according to verse one it is going to be in the desert of the sea. The Bible always refers to the Mediterranean Sea as the Great Sea, and the Dead Sea is always referred to as the Salt Sea, and the Red Sea as the Red Sea. But here it says "the desert of the sea." It is interesting that the Bible commentators even fifty and sixty years ago said it referred to the Persian Gulf. Isaiah 21:9 says:

*"Behold, here cometh a chariot of men, with a couple of horsemen."*

And, by the way, the latest tank of Israel is called

"The Chariot" tank. "The chariot of men, with a couple of horsemen. Babylon is fallen, is fallen . . ." implying again again, two fallings, one an ancient one under the Medes and Persians, and another which could be just around the corner.

Here's my question, are you ready for these coming events? Here's the story about a man who had a young family. The story is told that they were driving down the road one day when there was a terrible rainstorm. Because of the great rainstorm, the bridge had been washed away. And as this man drove along with his family trying to peer out the window, they didn't notice the bridge had been washed out. So his whole family and his car went over the edge of the road and into the river. Somehow or other he managed to escape from the car and made his way back to the shore and up to the road. There he tried with all his strength to stop every car that went by. He would watch as families would look at him as if to say, "Why is this man standing out here on the road in the middle of the rainstorm?" The kids would press their noses against the glass, but father and mother would speed along the road, and he would watch until the tail lights would disappear where the bridge had gone out. This man decided that he could stand it no longer, so he took off his coat, and there in the middle of the road he began to flag his coat in front of the next car that came. As the car came to a stop, the person in the car said, "Man, what are you doing out on a night like this?"

The man said, "The bridge is out! The bridge is out!" Quickly they got his car turned sideways to stop other traffic.

As we look at the events concerning Hussein, the war

in the Persian Gulf, and the end times, I really believe that the bridge is out. I believe that we are looking at the last few hours of the day and time that men and women, boys and girls can come to Christ. I wonder, what have you done with Christ? If I could, I'd like to take off my jacket today, and stand in front of all those people who would walk down life's highway, and I'd like to say, "Listen, the bridge is out! The bridge is out!" But, there is only one way that a person can bridge the gap to Heaven, and that is through the finished work of Jesus Christ. It says in 1 John 5:11-13:

> *"And this the record, that God hath given to us eternal life, and this life is in his Son. He that hath the Son hath life; and he that hath not the Son of God hath not life. These things have I written unto you that believe on the name of the Son of God, that ye may know that ye have eternal life."*

You see, the same God who promised each of these things that we've been reading about concerning Iraq and Babylon has also promised that any person who would come to Him by faith, and receive Christ, Christ would be their bridge.

So, today, are you really ready if Christ were to come? The Bible says that there will be a great time of excitement at the end of the church age, at the very end of the time we're living in right now. It says that Christ Himself will come in the clouds. The Bible says in 1 Thessalonians 4:16:

> *"For the Lord himself shall descend from*

*heaven with a shout, with the voice of the archangel, and with the trump of God: and the dead in Christ shall rise first: Then, we who are alive and remain shall be caught up together with them in the clouds, to meet the Lord in the air: and so shall we ever be with the Lord."*

What a great prospect this is! For every single person who acknowledges before God that they have sinned and that they have need of a Savior, God is willing to save them through the death of His Son, Jesus Christ. When Christ came into the world He had no sin of His own. So, when He died on the cross, He didn't die for His own sin, He died for my sin and your sin. The Bible says life is in Christ and if a person will accept Jesus Christ as the payment for their sin, His death on the cross, His shed blood, is sufficient to wash away, to cover, to put away our sin forever. The Bible says that anyone who will accept Christ can have that eternal life.

# *The Certainty Of Bible Prophecy*

Do you realize how interested people are in the future? Of all the things people read and think over, the future captivates their attention more than anything else.

How many of us have said, "Let's just watch the weather and then we'll go to bed." Now, why would you want to watch the weather? The guy's normally wrong. But we are so interested in the future, we'll even watch the weather, knowing the guy's wrong.

Millions of people begin every day by reading their horoscope. They'll read in the paper some fabricated story so general that anything that happens to them could fulfill it. Yet, nothing specific in a horoscope is ever, ever true. Why do people continue to read it? Because they want to know the future. Well, they won't find out about the future in a newspaper horoscope, but I know where they can.

The Bible is the book where God tells the future. The Bible is history written in advance, and it's signed and guaranteed by God.

On one occasion, a gypsy walked up to a believer and said, "If you'll cross my hand with a dollar, I'll tell you what's going to happen to you this time tomorrow." The believer said, "You can't do that." Then the gypsy replied, "If you'll cross my hand with a dollar, I'll show you." "No," the believer said. "How will I know that what you tell me will be true?" "You'll just have to wait and find out," the gypsy said. "I've got a better idea," the believer said. "I'll give you two dollars if you can tell me what was happening to me this time yesterday." The gypsy walked away.

There are a lot of people who will make a guess about the future, but the Scriptures give us the certainty of Bible prophecy. Matthew 24:35 says:

*"Heaven and earth shall pass away, but my words shall not pass away."*

His words, His predictions will not pass away.

Men can only guess at the future. We could bring the most brilliant military strategists here, and they could tell us what they *think* will happen in the Persian Gulf, but it may or may not come true.

But we can read chapter and verse in God's Word, and sooner or later (most probably sooner), it will come true exactly as God says it will happen. That's the certainty of Bible prophecy. We read in 2 Corinthians 1:20:

*"Every promise of God is yes, and in him guaranteed."*

2 Peter 1:19 states:

*"For we have a more sure word of prophecy."*

The test of prophecy when talking of the future comes down to: "Is the message valid?" Remember, when we read the Word of God, the authority of God is there.

Do you know the accuracy record of Old Testament Bible prophets compared to modern day so-called "prophets"?

Jean Dixon is right only five percent of the time when she predicts the future, and she makes a living at telling the future. Actually, she's wrong ninety-five percent of the time. Do you think that's a very good accuracy rate?

The marvel of Old Testament prophecy is that the prophets had to be right one hundred percent of the time. They had to be one hundred percent right, one hundred percent of the time. Deuteronomy 13:5-10 tells what happened if a prophet was wrong. It was gruesome. If a prophet made a proclamation that was wrong, they would strip him naked, tie his hands behind him, parade him outside the city, and walk him onto a platform. Then when the crowd gathered, they would push him off the platform, and the crowd would throw stones. The stones that took his life were separated out and used to mark his grave as one who thought he was a prophet and lied.

Today telling the future is big business, but it's not very accurate. I think we ought to require more of our prophets, don't you? I am not a prophet. I study Bible prophecy, and I pray, "Lord, keep me from making a prediction." Because I know that any prediction I make will more than likely be wrong unless it agrees exactly with God's Word.

Now the Bible, which is one hundred percent right one hundred percent of the time, has sixty-six sections. It was written by thirty different writers in three different languages over a period of sixteen hundred years. Every one of the messages in it agrees and brings together God's prophetic Word. The certainty of it marks God's Word as uniquely different from any other book in all the world.

It's not one book among many, it is the unique revelation of a God in control from the very beginning to the very end.

It doesn't matter if you take Daniel, Isaiah, Jeremiah, Micah, Amos, Zechariah, or Jesus because they were all prophets. The authority of God was invested in them so that not one prophecy in the Bible will ever go unfulfilled, and God gives His promise for that. I like that kind of prophecy, don't you?

In recent months, I have had a remarkable experience in terms of looking at an ongoing news event that appears to indicate that God's Word is being fulfilled. But other people get extremely nervous and have even said to me, "We really think that maybe you're getting a little too excited about relating current events to the Bible." My response is that I'm not sure that it's ever possible for someone to be too excited about the Bible.

There are a lot of things in life that you and I think are certain at the time. Sometimes we see a team play football, and we say, "That's a certain win." But then they lose. There's nothing really certain except the Word of God. It is important to realize that this book was written by God. And if God is God, and He is, then the Bible is as infallible as God. There's no man who is infallible, but God is. There's no book or history written that is perfectly correct other than the Bible. Count on it. God did write the Bible. The most risky thing we can do in life is not to believe the Bible.

I want to look at some of the predictions made by the Bible and how they have come true. As one begins to look at some of the prophecies, frankly, they look pretty foolish. Sometimes the accomplishment of the prophecy is against insurmountable odds, and sometimes it takes a long time for it all to be fulfilled. But every prophecy of God's Word that has been fulfilled has been fulfilled exactly as the Bible records it. Now that's quite a record, isn't it?

There are people who say they can predict that this person is going to do this, or this team is going to do that. People tend to take a lot of stock in those reports if the predictions are right sixty or seventy or eighty percent of the time. But what if the forecaster has a record so accurate that the prophecies are written as history? As we believe in the certainty of Bible prophecies, we begin to believe in the certainty of God. There is nothing in this world more important than the fact that God is in control.

If I were not a believer in Jesus Christ, I'd be real confused about what's going on in the Middle East. Many say that sooner or later there is going to be peace. I believe just the opposite, sooner or later there is going to be war. I'm not going to say that it's going to be at 12:01 on a certain date. It may not happen for a month or a year, but sooner or later what the Bible says about Iraq and Babylon will be exactly, literally, completely fulfilled. The most certain thing we can do is believe it. When it will occur is God's business, but believing it is our business.

In the Matthew 24:35 it says:

*"Heaven and earth shall pass away, but my words shall not pass away."*

These words are in the middle of a prophetic chapter. Jesus is saying that his prophecies will not pass away. That's quite a promise, isn't it?

When we get up in the morning, we really think that the sun is going to be up sooner or later. We expect it to go down, and we begin to believe that every day it is going to be the same. Jesus is saying that there is a better chance of Heaven and earth passing away than for even one single word of the Bible not to be fulfilled. Don't you like a God like that?

In 2 Corinthians 1:20, the Apostle Paul says:

*"For all the promises of God in him are yea, and in him Amen, unto the glory of God by us."*

In the Bible there are over seven thousand promises or predictions, and Paul says that every one is guaranteed. We like guarantees, especially if someone has the authority to back it up. God says that He wants you to know that every promise that He makes, every prophecy that He puts forward, He will fulfill. That's the certainty of God's Word.

2 Peter 1:19 says:

*"We have also a more sure word of prophecy; unto which you do well that you take heed, as unto a light that shines in a dark place, until the day dawn, and the day star arises in your hearts: Knowing this first, that no prophecy of the scripture is of any private interpretation. For the prophecy came not in old time by the will of man: but holy men of God spoke as they were moved by the Holy Spirit."*

The certainty of God's Word is expressed here in a

remarkable way. We need to realize that if a person speaks up and says, "God has given me a special revelation, none of you have seen this, but last night God spoke to me and He gave me this," we shouldn't believe it! Peter said that God spoke through the ancient men and that they recorded what He said. The Word that God has for us today is not because I have been given some special word. God has given me the same Word of God that's available to all — the Bible.

As we look at God's Word, Peter says there will be agreement. Next, it says that the Bible is of no private interpretation. He says that from Genesis to Revelation it must fit together, and it must make sense. We can't take a verse out of the middle and say, "This is what it means," and then build a whole doctrine on it. It must fit together. There must be continuity. Then Peter says that the men of old were moved by the Holy Spirit of God. Some incredible things were written by these men. To be honest, I don't think they actually understood all that they were writing.

The Apostle John wrote in Revelation about an army of two hundred million men marching from the East. Today we say that that's no problem because China can claim an army of two billion men. But we need to realize that at the time that John wrote those words there weren't even two billion men on the face of the earth.

Ezekiel wrote that there would be a great power named Rosh, or Russia. At the time of the writing, Russia was about as backward as a country could ever be. Ezekiel also wrote that the Roman Empire would be destroyed and that when we see a united Roman Empire coming back to power then we would know we are living in the last times. The Roman Empire cracked and crumbled, and who would ever have guessed that it would come back? These men wrote some incredible predictions, but the reason they could do so was because they were inspired by God. There's a certainty to Bible prophecy because it came from God.

There are always some people who will say, "The trouble is, how do you know that it applies to us today? How do you know that it's really being fulfilled now?" Those are valid questions. All we have to do is look at what God's Word says and if it has not been fulfilled yet, could it still be fulfilled in the future? The Bible has much to say about the future, and it applies to us today. It describes now and the next one thousand and seven years in the Word of God, and it talks about how God will then make a new Heaven and a new earth for those who have accepted Him.

I want to share with you some seemingly ridiculous promises of God and show you how God fulfilled them. Then I want to review some passages in Jeremiah to show you in detail how God described the situation that is taking place right now in the Middle East.

A prophecy of a long time ago is found in Ezekiel 26:4. This particular prophecy took a long time to prove. That's something people today can't handle very well. We're a generation that wants things *now*. We want an instant breakfast or an instant lunch, so we "drive-thru" the fast-food establishment, and we want our food *now*. If we go to a restaurant, and they take more than five minutes to serve us, the kids are saying, "What's wrong?" Five minutes isn't too bad to prepare a meal, but when we are used to the drive-thru's, it's tough.

Well, God is patient with His prophecies. Ezekiel

26:4,12 says:

> *"And they shall destroy the walls of Tyre, and break down her towers: I will also scrape the dust from her, and make her like the top of a rock. It shall be the place for the spreading of nets in the midst of the sea: for I have spoken it, saith the Lord God: and it shall become a spoil to the nations . . . And they shall make a spoil of thy riches, and make a prey of thy merchandise: and they shall break down the walls, and destroy thy pleasant houses: and they shall lay thy stones and thy timber and thy dust in the midst of the water."*

The powerful city named Tyre mentioned in this prophecy would be located today in Phoenicia or modern-day Lebanon. We can go back historically over fifteen hundred years and find and identify the city of Tyre. It was a powerful city with its own navy. Because the people of Tyre were on the coast of the Mediterranean Sea, they became rich people. The Bible records that they traded with David and with Solomon. But there came a time when Nebuchadnezzar, the king of Babylon, had the desire to gain control of them. He began to wage a war against Tyre. During the course of this battle, which lasted about thirteen years, Nebuchadnezzar sought after their riches to pay for his war campaign.

The pride of Tyre was incredible. They boasted that they could not be beaten. While Nebuchadnezzar could conquer Jerusalem and the surrounding cities, one city remained aloof to him. For thirteen years he battled Tyre and then he finally broke into the city. He discovered that the inhabitants had moved all their wealth, homes, and people to an island two thousand feet out into the sea. Nebuchadnezzar did not get one single spoil. He was so disappointed, so disgusted that he and the army went home having wasted thirteen years.

But Ezekiel said that Tyre would be destroyed. Looking at the battle of Nebuchadnezzar against Tyre and then looking at what God's Word says, we might question the fulfillment of God's prophecy if we had lived back then.

If I'd been living then, I'd have been a little frustrated and might have said, "He said He's going to break down the walls, He's going to scrape her like dust, He's going to make her like the top of a rock (some translations say "like the top of a table") and then He's going to take the riches and destroy their houses and put their dust in the water. But it didn't happen. What's the deal?"

So the prediction in God's Word to destroy Tyre and to lay Tyre flat as a rock with even the dust swept from her remained in God's Word unfulfilled.

Two hundred and fifty years after Nebuchadnezzar there was another man who sought to control and rule the world. His name was Alexander the Great. When he marched across the land conquering city after city, he came to Tyre whose people had returned to the mainland and rebuilt the city. When the people of Tyre saw Alexander coming, they quickly ran to the island. They reminded Alexander the Great that for thirteen years Nebuchadnezzar tried to conquer them, and he could never do it because on the island out in the middle of the ocean Tyre had a natural protection by huge cliffs. On top of those huge cliffs were huge walls that had kept Nebuchadnezzar from conquering Tyre.

When Alexander the Great came, however, within seven months he found a way to conquer the island. He had his soldiers go back to the deserted city, the city that was originally spoiled by Nebuchadnezzar, and take down the buildings, walls, and houses. They used the rocks to begin building a causeway, a road, from the mainland all the way to the island. In order to make their march on the island, the causeway was built two thousand feet long and two hundred feet wide. They used every rock, every piece of wood, anything to build that road through the water. They literally scraped the land clean to create the road. In seven months, Alexander the Great completely destroyed Tyre on the mainland and Tyre on the island.

Now look at God's Word. Was Ezekiel's prophecy fulfilled? Yes! God's Word was fulfilled exactly, *literally* as the Bible records it. The only thing was that it took two hundred fifty years for it to be fulfilled.

The Bible also says that Tyre would not be rebuilt. Since the destruction by Alexander the Great some twenty-three hundred years ago, there certainly has been plenty of time for it to have been rebuilt, but it has not been. Do you know what it is used for today? The fishermen of the area come and spread their nets over this area that has been left flat for these twenty-three hundred years. What did the Bible predict? Tyre would not be rebuilt, it would be destroyed, and fishermen would spread their nets. It says that even the debris would be used to be put in the water for the road. I think we can count on the certainty of Bible prophecy.

I admit that it took a long time to fulfill it, but God is patient. The proof of His patience is our salvation. For nineteen hundred years God has been begging men and women to come and to receive the finished work of Christ on the cross. Have you ever done it? During your lifetime, God has been patiently bringing the gospel before you again and again. He's waiting for you to come to Him.

God is not changed by our ideas of what the time frame should be for an event. At the appropriate time, God's Word was and will be literally and actually fulfilled. You see the certainty of God's Word knowing that it will be fulfilled exactly as God says. I think it's great to live with that kind of certainty.

Sometimes we forget that the familiar stories of the Bible are actually predictions by God. For example, Genesis 6:3-4:

*"And the Lord said, My spirit shall not always strive with man, for that he is also flesh: yet his days shall be a hundred and twenty years."*

It goes on to tell of giants in the land and a mixing of the races. Then we read Genesis 6:5-7:

*"And God saw that the wickedness of man was great in the earth, and that every imagination of the thoughts of his heart was only evil continually. And it repented the Lord that he had made man on the earth, and it grieved him at his heart. And the Lord said, I will destroy man whom I have created from the face of the earth; both man, and beast, and the creeping thing and*

*the fowls of the air; for it repenteth me that I have made them."*

God pronounced the judgment that He would destroy the man and beasts which He made. He then begins by telling Noah to build an ark.

The thing that's ridiculous about that, first of all, is that Noah probably wasn't even very close to the ocean. Can't you see Noah one afternoon beginning the project out there in the back yard. Mrs. Noah hears a bunch of hammering and sawing and goes out and asks Noah what he's doing. "I'm building an ark," he responds. "Oh, that's nice, is that like a picnic table?" she asks. "Well, no. This thing floats," Noah answers. "Well, that's nice, too, but why do we need one of those?" she asks. Noah begins to answer, "Well, you see, a rain, a huge rain . . ." "What's rain?" Noah's wife asks in wonder.

You see, so far in history it had never rained. How could they understand about a flood if it had never rained? Don't you think that there would be a few reasons for Noah to question what God had spoken? But he didn't. If Noah had questioned the certainty of what God promised, Noah would have been destroyed.

What if Noah had listened to all the logic of his critics? It says in Hebrews 11:7:

*"Noah believed things not yet seen."*

I think that would be hard to do. But here's Noah who has to believe in a flood, and it has never flooded. He has to believe in rain, and it has ever rained. He has to build a huge boat, and he has never designed or built a huge boat, and he has to do it with just three of his sons with all the rest of the world mocking him. Hard business, wasn't it?

So here's Noah, and God speaks to him, "Here's what's going to happen. I'm going to give you a plan for a boat. It's going to flood, it's going to rain, and I want you to take two of every kind of animal, and seven of the clean ones, and I want you to load them in the ark and just trust me."

God said to begin building and that in one hundred twenty years, judgment was going to come. I can see getting all excited about this thing and then about two years into the project, Noah's boys say, "This boat is huge; it's gigantic. Dad, are you really sure God told you this, or did you just have a bad dream? Dad, does this thing have to be so big? Why can't we have normal life? Dad, I'd like to play sports after school, but every night I've got to come home and work on the ark. We're going to work on this for one hundred and twenty years! Can't we quit for a while?"

All the neighbors met on a regular basis to harrass him according to the Bible. That was their entertainment. They didn't have television. "Let's go watch Noah." They would harrass him and catcall to him, "What are you going to build next?" I think it took a lot of faith on Noah's part to continue building.

I believe if we today trust in the certainty of God's Word, there will be people who are going to mock us. We have to decide either to believe them or to believe God.

I can see the people as Noah and his family moved into the ark. Not only would it be discouraging to have all the people harrassing him for one hundred twenty years, but as he built the ark, it says in verse twenty-two that Noah obeyed the Lord in all the things that He told him to do. After he completed the ark, he went in with the animals and his family and shut the door. For a period of time they were sitting there with all the harrassers outside and no rain or flood came, probably not even any clouds were in the sky. I can hear the people saying, "Come on Noah, give it up, get out! Noah, come on, we won't tease you too much!" Don't you think it would have been tempting to say, "All right, come on, enough is enough," and then to have walked right out of there?

The whole thing began to change when the first heckler said, "Who spit on me?" Another guy said, "I don't know, but someone just spit on me, too. Hey, stop!" All of a sudden, "What is that?" "I don't know, but it kind of feels good." They let the rain fall on their faces. It rained a little longer. "Hey, while you guys are bothering Noah, I'm going to go back and shut the windows." I can see this guy going back and saying, "You know, this is strange. Whatever this is, it has never happened before." The wife responded, "What is happening to my laundry? Look at it out there on the line." Suddenly, they began to make a few changes, didn't they?

And it didn't stop raining. Can't you see those people walking around to each other's houses with the water about knee deep? Now, instead of jeers and mocking, there was a little concern. Can't you see those poor families, as the water in the house gets to be about neck deep, running to the ark and pounding on it? "Noah! Noah! Noah, let us in! Noah, we didn't mean it! Noah, if you know something we don't know, let us in!" That has to be one of the most frightening scenes ever portrayed in the Bible.

But there's Noah and his family and a few people that believed the certainty of God's promise. They were the only ones that were saved. I'm so glad that Noah trusted in the certainty of God's prediction. It was ridiculous, but it was true. We have God's Word today, and I don't care how long it takes to be fulfilled, sooner or later, God's Word will be fulfilled.

I don't care how ridiculous it may look, God's Word is sure. It's a sure word of prophecy. *"Heaven and earth shall pass away, my words shall not pass away,"* said Jesus in Matthew 24:35. *"For we have a more sure word of prophecy: whereunto ye do well that ye take heed, as unto a light that shineth in a dark place,"* states 1 Peter 1:19. Every promise of God in Him is yea, in Him guaranteed by the glory of God. Sooner or later His glory will shine.

In Joshua 3:3-4 is what looks like a foolish plan. You might have said, "If we're going to do something silly, let's not make it quite so obvious."

> *"And they commanded the people, saying, When ye see the ark of the covenant of the Lord your God, and the priests the Levites bearing it, then ye shall remove from your place, and go after it. Yet there shall be a space between you and it, about two thousand cubits by measure: come not near unto it, that ye may know the way by which ye must go: for ye have not passed this way heretofore."*

In other words, this is brand new territory. We continue with verse 5:

*"And Joshua said unto the people, Sanctify yourselves: for tomorrow the Lord will do wonders among you."*

Joshua told them, "When you see the battle plan, you're not going to believe it, just trust me." Joshua 6:2 says:

*"And the Lord said to Joshua, See, I have given into thine hand Jericho, and the king thereof, and the mighty men of valour."*

Of all the cities in the promised land, the one that was the most frightening to go up against was Jericho. It had a huge wall, a fierce king, and a mighty army. But God said, "Joshua, look at that city, it's already conquered." And there's Joshua looking at the wall that was still standing. "No," God said, "that city's already conquered. I've given you the city. I've given you the king. I've given you the whole army."

Do you realize that Israel had not fought a battle in some four hundred forty years. They were slaves for four hundred years. They had been marching for forty, and now they were going up against the strongest city around. And the Lord said, "Joshua, they're yours, because I have already promised that they will be defeated. Now, here's the plan."

I can see Joshua saying, "Man, now I'm going to find out the design of those M-16s!" But the Lord said, "I want you to take the priests and the ark and begin to walk around the city one time the first day. But, don't say anything."

Now, that's the best part, the only part I can understand in the whole battle plan. I know that if He had let them talk they would have grumbled the whole way.

I can also see the people of Jericho up on the wall saying, "You Jews are crazy!" And they were probably telling Jew jokes — you can imagine the harrassment. All Joshua and the people did was march. At the end of one time around, they went back to their tents, and that was that. That was an impressive battle plan, wasn't it? A neat way to conquer a huge, mighty city with great walls, right?

Guess what they did the next day? You'll like this one. They got up, the priests went with the ark, and they went around the city one time without saying one word. That would frighten the enemy, wouldn't it? On the third day came the truly unique part of the plan. They got up and followed the ark all the way around the city without saying a word just like the day before. They did this for a whole week! About then, what would you have been doing? I think you would have been saying, "You know what, Joshua, I don't think this is going to work. We're scary, but I don't think we're that scary. Do you have any other plan?" Joshua would have responded, "Yes, now we are going to go around the city seven times." I don't mind telling you, this looks like a ridiculous prophecy. But when the whole thing was done, at the end of those seven times, God told Joshua to declare the city as theirs. He told them to stand and yell, and the walls of the city would collapse. And it happened just that way!

In the past year in the public paper there was a statement concerning, "No more laughing about Jericho." Do you want to know why? Archaeology has discovered that the walls fell exactly as the Bible said they did.

God said that's what would happen, and it was fulfilled literally. I don't care how foolish it sounds, I don't care how much mocking we get. I don't care how long it takes, if God says it will happen — it will happen! There was a marvelous fulfillment of what God had predicted in Exodus 12:41:

> *"And it came to pass at the end of the four hundred and thirty years, even the very same day it came to pass, that all the hosts of the Lord went out from the land of Egypt."*

Four hundred and thirty years earlier in Genesis 10, God said, "Abraham, I want you to know that I'm going to deliver you out of Egypt." Then, thirty years later, in Genesis 15:13, He said, "Abraham, I don't know if you are keeping track, but in four hundred years I promise I'm going to deliver you out of Egypt." So, when God finally delivered Israel, do you remember how He did it? It was a mighty plan. They gathered together and marched straight for the sea, and God parted the sea with a strong wind. Now is that how you would have gotten across the sea? It looked like insurmountable odds. They escaped from the Egyptians, the most powerful army in all the world, and they didn't have a single weapon. The Jews were spared, and the Egyptians were drowned. The certainty of God's Word! And it happened on the very day that God said it would. I'm so glad they trusted in what some would have thought to be a ridiculous prophecy.

Even when it seems contradictory, God still fulfills His prophecy. 2 Kings 24:17-20 contains a marvelous story which shows the validity of the Bible:

*"And the kings of Babylon made Mattaniah his father's brother king in his stead, and changed his name to Zedekiah. Zedekiah was twenty and one years old when he began to reign, and he reigned eleven years in Jerusalem. And his mother's name was Hamutal, the daughter of Jeremiah of Libnah. And he did that which was evil in the sight of the Lord, according to all that Jehoiakim had done."*

It goes on to tell how Zedekiah rebelled against the king of Babylon. Now some history takes place between verses nineteen and twenty. Nebuchadnezzar destroyed one king, took him back as a captive, and then sets up Zedekiah as king. As king, he said, "You know, I think I like this position. Instead of giving taxes back to Nebuchadnezzar, I'm going to keep the taxes for myself." As he thought these things, two prophets began to write against him. One was the prophet Jeremiah. In Jeremiah 32:3-4, we read:

*"And Zedekiah king of Judah had shut him up, saying, Why dost thou prophesy, and say, Thus saith the Lord, Behold, I will give this city into the hand of the king of Babylon, and he shall take it; And Zedekiah king of Judah shall not escape out of the hand of the Chaldeans, but shall surely be delivered into the hand of the king of Babylon, and shall speak with him mouth to mouth, and his eyes shall behold his eyes."*

The prophet Jeremiah said, "Listen, you're going to

get into trouble. You're going to be taken captive. You're going to be delivered to the king of Babylon. And you're going to see him face to face."

The trouble was, there was another prophet named Ezekiel who began to warn this willful king by saying, "Don't you realize that you're going contrary to the plan and authority of god?" Here's his prediction in Ezekiel 12:13:

*"My net also will I spread upon him, and he shall be taken in my snare: I will bring him to Babylon to the land of the Chaldeans; yet shall he not see it, though he shall die there."*

Then Zedekiah says, "See, that's the trouble with prophecy. You guys can't agree. One prophet says I'm going to be taken and delivered to the king, and the other one says, no, you're not going to see Babylon at all. I don't think either one of you knows what he's talking about. I'm going to do what I want to do."

2 Kings 25:6 says they took him captive and brought him first to the king of Babylon. There they brought his two sons in and slaughtered them and gouged out his eyes. The last sight he would ever see would be his sons killed. He'd never forget it. Then they brought him blinded into Babylon where he was a prisoner until he died.

Zedekiah had said, "I don't think Jeremiah and Ezekiel know what they're talking about. They're giving contradictory prophecies." But even prophecies that seem contradictory will be fulfilled just as God says they will. How could Zedekiah be brought to see the king and not see Babylon? How would he never see Babylon and yet die there? Here's how. He would be taken captive, and be brought to another city to meet the king. He would have his eyes gouged out and then be brought to Babylon where he would wait to die. That's exactly what happened. God has a certainty in His Word.

Jeremiah 50:1 contains passages of scripture that have come alive to us in the past few months. First, in verse one, *"The word that the Lord spoke against Babylon. . . ."* Whether we like it or not, God's Word has a word against Babylon, and modern-day Iraq is nothing more than ancient Babylon. As we see the prophecies spoken by God against Babylon, I think they apply to Iraq today because it is the same land.

It's the Word of the Lord. It's His plan. It's not the plan and the word of George Bush. It's not the word of America. God doesn't need America to bring punishment to Iraq, for He'll do it any way He wants to. Frankly, before the whole thing is completed, it may be Israel that does the work.

Here's what it says in verse two: *"Declare ye among the nations, and publish, and set up a standard; publish, and conceal not. . . ."* He said, "Listen, this isn't any private prophecy to threaten Iraq. This thing is to be released, to be declared among people to set a standard. Conceal it not. Let the people know."

Someone has already told me that I'm for war. No, I'm not. I am for the plan of God, whatever it is. And if that's war, then bring on war. If that's peace, let's have peace.

The Bible has many wars that are still predicted. The Bible says there will be a battle between Russia and Israel — it will come. The Bible says when Russia and desperately needs food, when they need money, they'll invade Israel. You think it will happen? I know it will occur. Ask Colonel Yehuda Levy, "Do you think there will be a battle between Russia and Israel?" He says, "I know there will be a battle." Ask former Prime Minister Rabin, and he says, "I know there will be a battle." Why? Because these people believe the certainty of Bible prophecy. The only ones that doubt seem to be supposed Christians who say they believe the Bible.

The war between Israel and Russia is yet in the future. Russia has never invaded Israel. That battle is just as sure as anything we've already seen because God's Word records it. The Bible talks of the Battle of Armageddon. That's a future war. Before you say that it's crazy to claim that the Bible is predicting wars for today. Just remember the Bible says there will be wars and rumors of wars. The Bible says all the nations will surround Israel and if it wasn't for God's intervention, the world would collapse and devour Israel. The Bible has much to say about future wars. It says in Zechariah 14 to proclaim it openly, and that's what I'm trying to do.

Looking at recent events in light of prophecy, how does Kuwait figure into it? Look at Jeremiah 49:20. It says that "the least of the flock shall draw them out." I've thought often that that might be Israel, but frankly I'm changing my mind. Maybe it's Kuwait, because I've noticed in chapter 49:20, and 50:45 that the nation used to expose Iraq will be desolate and destroyed. In 50:8 it says that many will leave the country:

> *"Flee out of the midst of Babylon, and go forth*
> *out of the land of the Chaldeans. . . ."*

Isn't that what's been happening? Chapter 51:6 says:

*"Flee out of the midst of Babylon, and deliver every man his soul. . . ."*

And we've watched as the people fled the country. What about the hostages? Jeremiah 50:37 says that Iraq will take a mingled people, a mixture of people, and they will hold them. What about the embargo? Chapter 50:9 states:

*"I will raise and cause to come up against Babylon an assembly of great nations. . . ."*

Are they there? They sure are. One of the most unprecedented moves by the United Nations was for the nations to band together and to hold together in the last hours of the so-called peace talks. It seems incredible. Jeremiah 50:16 says:

*"Cut off the sower from Babylon, and him that held the sickle in the time of harvest: for fear of the oppressing sword they shall turn every one to his people, and they shall flee every one to his own land."*

There will be people there and they will flee to their land. This has happened.

How does Israel come into all of it? Look at Jeremiah 50:17:

*"Israel is a scattered sheep; the lions have driven him away."*

It introduces Israel and says there will be punishment (v, 18) upon the king of Babylon.

Frankly, as you look at the threats of Hussein, they really do make quite a scenario. *Time* magazine quotes:

*"I swear to God we will let our fire eat half of Israel if it tries to wage anything against Iraq."*

The date of the article is April 16, 1990, about five months before the invasion. No threat by Israel. *Newsweek*, August 13, 1990 says, "Target Jerusalem." *Newsweek* says, "Could the real prize be Jerusalem and not Kuwait at all?" The *New York Times*, page A14, August 13, 1990, "Saddam's Next Target, Israel." Hussein said:

*"If anyone attacks us, including the United States, for any reason, we go after Israel."*

We don't know how it will all happen, but I believe the whole thing is called into question to make it an Arab-Israeli conflict instead of Hussein on a solo mission. But the Bible is very clear it will happen because of the pride and the arrogance of the king of Iraq. He has the arrogance. It's not polite to criticize political leaders, but I'm one person who does not think that Hussein is an asset to the world.

The *Los Angeles Times* in September 1990 quoted Hussein saying:

*"With the right chemicals and the right place we can destroy ninety-eight percent of Israel with one hit if the wind is right."*

The Bible says in Jeremiah 51:1-2:

*"Thus saith the Lord; Behold, I will raise up against Babylon, and against those that dwell in the midst of them that rise up against me, a destroying wind* [the wind will figure into the battle]. *And will send into Babylon winnowers, that shall fan her, and shall empty her land: for in the day of trouble they shall be against her round about."*

He will use the wind and the same chemical warfare that Hussein would like to use on Israel. When those chemicals come against Israel, I wouldn't be a bit surprised if the winds change, and it ends up destroying Iraq. That's what the Bible says — a strong wind, a destroying wind. I believe it might come back on Mr. Hussein.

Jeremiah 51:9 says:

*"We would have healed Babylon, but she is not healed: forsake her, and let us go every one into his own country. . . ."*

He said that there was a chance for peace, but they would not accept the peace. I've never seen more people, more nations make more concessions to a king and have him refuse to accept peace. And when it's all done, chapter 51:43-44 says there will be a day that the same king who refuses peace will repent and regret the decision he made. I think it will be fulfilled completely, accurately just as God says.

Look at the tragedy of it in Jeremiah 5:13:

*"Because of the wrath of the Lord it shall not be inhabited, but it shall be wholly desolate: every one that goeth by Babylon shall be astonished, and hiss at her plagues."*

Has that ever happened? Absolutely not. It has never been destroyed in that fashion. Look at verses 21-23:

*"Go up against the land of Merathaim, even against it, and against the inhabitants of Pekod: waste and utterly destroy after them, said the Lord. . . . A sound of battle is in the land, and of great destruction. How is the hammer of the whole earth cut asunder and broken! how is Babylon become a desolation among the nations!"*

How in the world could the destruction be so complete, so total? Verses twenty-six through thirty-two give the description of the violence in the war that takes place, and we find that those weapons have never yet been used on planet earth. But in verse thirty, we read:

*"Therefore shall her young men fall in the streets, and all her men of war shall be cut off in that day, saith the Lord."*

Has that occurred? Has the entire army of Iraq been wiped out? Not yet. I don't care how foolish it may sound or how much we may be mocked or how long it takes, sooner or later it will be fulfilled exactly.

Jeremiah 51:8 says:

*"Babylon is suddenly fallen and destroyed: wail for her; take balm for her pain, if so she may be healed."*

It continues to say that it will be like the desolation of Sodom and Gomorrah. It will be so destroyed, so burnt, and so desolate that no man or animal can live there. This is exactly the scenario that would happen if anthrax and other chemical warfare were used.

Next we read Jeremiah 51:48-49:

*"Then the heaven and the earth, and all that is therein, shall sing for Babylon: for the spoilers shall come unto her from the north, saith the Lord. As Babylon has caused the slain of Israel to fall, so at Babylon shall fall the slain of all the earth."*

In other words, the battle that will be there will involve more than just Iraq, or Babylon, but all the earth will have soldiers there, and death will be present in every nation. Verse 62:

*"Then shall thou say, O Lord, thou hast spoken against this place, to cut it off, that none shall remain in it, neither man nor beast, but that it shall be desolate for ever."*

Once it is destroyed, it will never be rebuilt. That has

never been fulfilled yet. It may seem foolish to some, but before God is done, it will be literally fulfilled. Now, I can't say that it's going to take place today or tomorrow or this summer or next fall, but sooner or later this passage will be exactly, completely fulfilled. Why? Because God's Word is a sure word of prophecy. That's what we know.

If I had a son or daughter or relative there, I would be very concerned because God's Word is very specific that many young men will die. This man fought a war for eight years, spent $112 billion, lost forty thousand men in one battle, and he claims he won the war. He has wiped out several of his own villages and his own people testing his chemical weapons. In one case he said they deserved it. A man with this kind of mentality, or lack thereof, is liable to do the most bizarre things.

Why can't we just ignore all of this? All the time countries swallow up another country, so when Iraq swallowed up Kuwait, why didn't we just ignore it? While we've all been concentrating on Kuwait and Iraq, Syria has taken Lebanon. That's no more fair than taking Kuwait, but we ignore it. The president says we can no longer ignore Iraq because to bring in the "New World Order," Hussein must be gotten rid of.

It will bring in the "New World Order." Whether we like it or not, what the Bible predicts is exactly true, and America and Iraq are simply carrying out what the Word of God has already said will be the basic desires and the direction of the man called the Antichrist. The plan is fully in effect. We can try to ignore it, but it doesn't change the certainty of the Bible, does it?

Why does God give us prophecy? Why did He give a

prophetic warning to the people of Noah's day? Because he knew that there would be some people who would listen and come to believe it. His patience in these days may not be so much for Iraq as it is for us that we might begin to see the certainty of God's Word.

We talk of thousands of young men that will die. We talk of whole nations that will be wiped out. And as you look at God's Word, it also says that Israel will sign a peace treaty. Do you think that Israel today would sign a treaty as long as Hussein is in Iraq armed the way he is? There's not a chance. The Bible says when Russia comes to Israel, Iran will join and then Russia, but Iraq won't. Why? Could it be that Iraq will have been destroyed, completely, literally, as the Bible says? I think it might be.

We may see the literal fulfillment of this passage of Scripture because God says, "When I'm done, all the world will say, 'It was God who did this.'" He says in verse twenty: "I will use Israel as my battle axe." That's what He literally says, and that's why I believe sooner or later Israel will be involved in the whole plan. Verse 20:

*"Thou are my battle axe and weapons of war:*
*for with thee will I break in pieces the nations,*
*and with thee will I destroy kingdoms."*

Sooner or later Israel will get involved, whether it wants to or not. If Israel is involved, there could be the use of nuclear weapons to at least a limited degree.

Carl Sagan is not one of my favorite scientists, but on a recent television appearance he had a brilliant deduction. He said, "I'm no longer afraid of AIDS. I'm no longer afraid of banks failing. I'm not even afraid of war in the

Persian Gulf." He was discussing a new book he has written that they won't let him publish because he's using confidential information. In this new book, he talks about a nuclear winter. On television he said that if there would be a nuclear blast on a large oil field or a large oil refinery, and it would actually produce soot. It would be hard to confine, especially with a nuclear blast. It would form a whole soot cloud around enough of the earth to lower the temperature thirty to seventy degrees, and we would freeze. "Do you realize," he said, "that if a nuclear war breaks out right now in Kuwait we could lose, by starvation, a billion people, a fourth of the world?"

I thought, "I've never known Sagan to quote the Bible." But I quickly turned to Revelation 6 where the Tribulation begins. You know what happens? Death comes as a fourth of all the people starve. You never know what God will do with pagan Sagan. I don't care what point of view you come from, sooner or later God's Word is going to be fulfilled exactly as He said. I can't promise a nuclear winter, I can't say there'll be an attack today or tomorrow. Here's all I know, sooner or later Babylon will be destroyed exactly as God said, destroyed and never rebuilt. No man or animal will ever live there again. How can I say this? Because of the certainty of Bible prophecy.

Here's the challenge of it. If this battle takes place tomorrow or next week, are you ready? That's the question. If this battle takes place next month, are you ready? For some of you, I believe you really need to see there's another great promise made by God's Word. Do you know what it is? John 3:36 says:

*"He that has the Son has life."*

That's a prophecy of God. God predicted that anyone who trusts in Him will have eternal life. That's a certain prophecy! That's as good as done. It's so good as done, He said that if you'll believe Him right now, He'll give you eternal life right now. That's my favorite prophecy in all the Bible — eternal life. It goes on to say that he that has "not the Son shall not see life; but the wrath of God abideth on him." His other promise is that those who have not received Christ will meet with the judgment of God.

Also, there's nothing in the Bible that says that we have to wait until after the war breaks out for the Rapture. We could be raptured today, and the war could break out tomorrow. Here's the question, are you ready? I believe that we may see the conflict. When it comes, I believe that God's Word will be fulfilled so literally that Peter Jennings, Dan Rather, Ted Koppel, and all the others will say, "You want to know something? That's exactly what God said would take place." That's what the Bible says all the world will know. "The Lord's Word was fulfilled." Proclaim it! We may be mocked, but the Word of God cannot be mocked because it's a certain, sure Word of prophecy. Where do you stand? Do you really believe it?

The Bible promises life to those who accept it and eternal death to those who don't. The challenge of Bible prophecy is to live in view of the fact that Christ is coming soon. All the time people say, "Yeah, I know the Lord is coming sometime, but how do I know it will be in my lifetime?" When Jesus came the first time people were saying the same thing. All of the Jews were waiting for the Messiah, weren't they? When Jesus finally came, not very many said, "It'll be in my lifetime." Christ's second coming has to be in someone's lifetime, and I think it might be in ours. Are you ready if Christ were to come today?

# The Calamity Of Bible Prophecy

We need to understand that when God's Word speaks, it carries with it the authority of God Himself. There is calamity associated with Bible prophecy.

Recently I've spoken with people who say, "I just don't believe God could ever be mad enough to bring war on the earth." Well, if you believe the Bible applies to us today as I do, then there is no doubt that there will be wars. What we've been seeing in the Persian Gulf War, with all of its horror, its devastation, is only the beginning of what God has in store for planet earth.

Now, you should know that there is hope in the cross of Jesus Christ. That is the Grand Message. If there was not salvation in Jesus Christ, I, for one, would not want to tell you about what the future has in store. But there is eternal life by coming to Jesus Christ.

Luke 14:15 gives us a parable that illustrates the calamity of His coming. Parables were used by God to drive home a strong point.

> "Now when one of them that sat eating with Him heard these things, he said unto him, Blessed is he that shall eat bread in the kingdom of God. Then said he unto him, a certain man made a great supper, and bade many [invited many]: and sent his servant at supper time to say to them that they were bidden, Come; for all

*things are now ready. And they all with one consent began to make excuse. The first said unto him, I have bought a piece of ground, and I must needs to and see it: I pray thee have me excused. And another said, I have bought five yoke of oxen, and I go to prove them: I pray thee, have me excused. And another said, I have married a wife, and therefore I cannot come. So the servant came, and showed his lord these things. Then the master of the house being angry said to his servant, Go out quickly into the streets and lanes of the city, and bring in here the poor, and the maimed, and the halt, and the blind. And the servant said, Lord, it is done as thou hast commanded, and yet there is room. And the Lord said unto the servant, Go out into the highways and hedges, and compel them to come in, that my house may be filled. For I say unto you, that none of those men which were bidden shall taste of my supper."*

The calamity of His coming. You might think that if the world got a glimpse of the One who could say something and keep His word, they would be so thrilled that they immediately would come to Christ. Why wouldn't a person come to Christ when they finally find a source that is true? I've always dreamed of a time when someone would come up to me and say, "I want to be saved." This past week, I got a phone call from a man who didn't say, "Hello." He didn't say, "Who is this?" He just said, "I want to be saved." When the secretary told me, "There's someone on the phone who wants to be saved," I couldn't wait to get on the phone. You would think there would be hundreds and thousands of people wanting to be saved when they see what's happening in today's world.

What we saw in Iraq was a Sunday school picnic compared to what God is going to bring on planet earth in the future. That's the calamity of Bible prophecy. If people are afraid when they see this little war, just wait until the Tribulation, wait until they begin to see the judgment of God poured out on all the earth. There is calamity in not accepting forgiveness and salvation in Christ.

A great theologian said, "Don't scare people." I believe God will bring His judgment upon this man who's afraid to pronounce the coming of a great judgment day. There's nothing that sends people to Hell faster than saying, "My friend, you're all right just the way you are."

Matthew 22:2 says: *". . . a certain king made a marriage for his son."* Many were invited. The coming of Christ is really the marriage of God's Son, Jesus Christ, to those who have received Him by faith. Now if I had my choice between a wedding and the Tribulation, I know which I'd choose to attend. Can you imagine a great king arranging a marriage for his son, and you receive an invitation, and then you don't go?

This particular calamity is preceded by great preparation. Luke 14:16 tells of a great supper to which many were invited by the king. Can you imagine the cleaning that must have gone on around the palace. They probably cleaned places that were already clean. And the great invitations went out. Luke 14:17 says: *". . . Come; for all things are now ready."* Things are ready today, too.

I really believe that Christ could come at any minute. At this time, our eyes are focused on war. But if you have accepted Christ as Savior, you ought to have one eye on the Lord's coming, and the other eye on the Lord's coming, too. The war is God's way of getting the attention of men and women. It's His way of saying that because of sin there will be continual war. My eyes are on the clouds because He's coming in the clouds. One of these days, we're going to hear the sound of a trumpet, and the Christians will be gone. Then the whole world is going to know what wars really are. But there won't be Christians left to be on their knees praying for the safety of men in conflict. There won't be Christians praying for officials to make a proper decision.

Here's the grand invitation: "Come, for all things are now ready." Do you know that there's not one verse that says that Christians have to be here when all of chapters fifty and fifty-one of Jeremiah are completed? We could be raptured before they are fully completed as God's Word says. I think the Lord could come today. The battle may not be done before tomorrow, but the Lord could come today. The question is, are *you* ready?

Then at the invitation in Luke 14:17 there were the gross excuses. They were ridiculous! This is the king's son getting married! This is a great dinner! One man when invited, said, "I would like to come, but it just so happens that I've just bought some land. This is a major investment, you know. What I really need to do instead of going to dinner tonight at the marriage of the king's son is to look over my land." What in the world could he see about that land at night? Is that land going to change between night and morning? This guy's concerned with his wealth. Don't you think that's a ridiculous excuse? What's your excuse for not coming to Christ?

Another man said, "I've bought five yoke of oxen. I need to go out and test them." Can't you see these oxen with headlights on, and he's testing them to see if he got stuck with a bad deal? Couldn't he wait until morning?

So, the first man's concerned with his wealth, the second man's concerned with his oxen, and another man is concerned with his wife. He'd like to come, but with a new marriage and a new wife, he can't come. Why not invite her? All of these excuses when looked at closely look pretty thin.

What's your excuse for not coming to Christ? Whatever it is, it doesn't hold up very well when viewed in the light of eternity, does it?

Then there's a great proclamation in verse 244: ". . . *none of those men which were bidden shall taste of my supper.*" There was no second chance. It will be the same in days to come. Those that had the chance to come and did not come will not be saved in the Tribulation period. Now that's harsh. If you've heard the gospel and understand the claims of Christ and do not receive Christ, I really believe you will never receive Him, according to 2 Thessalonians 2:12. That's serious. When God opens the door and invites people in, and they say no, for whatever reason, it's not a good reason. The calamity of the Bible is that it brings judgment upon those who do not receive the message.

Many today preach, "Well, if you come, great, and if not, that's all right." But I believe that with God, it's a pressing issue.

Years ago, when Queen Elizabeth was crowned, they

sent out invitations to people that were poor and people that were rich, some that were in government, and some that were not, and people from all walks of life. The invitations were marvelous. Everyone was excited wondering if they would be among those invited. Wouldn't it be spectacular to be invited to a coronation like that? At the bottom of the invitation, it said, "All excuses ceasing." They accepted no excuses. You were invited; you be there. Now if that's for the Queen of England, can you imagine when it's the King of kings sending the invitation? All excuses ceasing. Whatever in the world would keep you from accepting Christ?

The calamity of Bible prophecy is that sometimes people don't understand it. We begin to think that life's just about as bad as it can be. But let me take you on a little tour in Revelation 4 and show you what the Bible predicts is ahead. By the way, one of the ways that I know that this will come true exactly as God recorded it is that the Apostle John has seen every one of the things recorded in Revelation. So if he has already seen it, it's as good as done.

Revelation 4:1 says:

*"After this I looked, and behold, a door was opened in heaven: and the first voice which I heard was as it were of a trumpet talking with me; which said, Come up here, and I will show you things which must be hereafter."*

He's going to get a glimpse of the future. He's going to actually see the things which will take place in the future. And when the trumpet sounds, with the invitation to go up and join with Christ, I believe that's the coming of Christ called "the Rapture of believers." At that time, everyone who has received Christ will go to be with Jesus. Here's the important question. Will you be among those raptured? It doesn't matter if you are a church member or a member of fifteen different churches and you tithe to every one of them. That will not get you into Heaven. It doesn't matter if you've been baptized forward, backward, sideways, and sprinkled six other times. It doesn't make you saved. It doesn't matter if you've read the Bible in Hebrew, English, and French. And even if you can say John 3:16 backward, it doesn't make you saved.

Do you have Christ as your personal Savior? If you do, then when Christ comes, He'll take you to be with Him. If you don't, when He comes you'll be riveted to the pew. When Christ comes and takes home believers, the scene portrayed in Revelation 4 and 5 is a grand one, a glorious one. As we meet Christ face to face, and we worship Him, the thrill and the joy of that is beyond compare. But when you come to Revelation 6:1-2, a whole new scene opens. The Tribulation begins after the Rapture of the church.

There are twenty-one judgments listed in Revelation. When you get through the first seven, called seals, there are seven judgments called trumpets. After the seven trumpets, seven bowls will be poured out, for a total of twenty-one judgments upon the earth.

In Revelation 6:1-2, He breaks the first seal revealing suddenly the Antichrist. The Antichrist comes forward with a peace treaty and a New World Order. Now, I don't mind telling you that as proud as I am of our president for taking a stand in the Middle East with Iraq, every time he says we're doing this in the name of the "New World Order," I shudder. The reason that they must do away with Hussein is because he does not subcribe to the New World Order. Now that's exactly what the Bible says will happen. In the end they will try to bring everyone together under a peace treaty and instead of peace, there will be war. The Bible talks about the New World Order, but it's not endorsed by God. I believe that among the things that had to happen to bring it about was the removal of Margaret Thatcher. And I wouldn't be surprised if Hussein is removed.

The Bible says that part of this New World Order will eventually be Israel signing a peace treaty and setting down its weapons. Right now, the most unlikely nation in all the world to set down its weapons is Israel. Do you think you could go over to Israel today and negotiate a peace contract? You might be a good salesman, but you'd never get it done. But when Iraq is destroyed, and Hussein is dethroned, Israel will say, "Maybe there is a New World Order." The Bible says these will be the conditions. But the problem is that according to verse three, as soon as the treaty is signed, the second seal breaks, and wars comes out. But God wanted man to fight war under His plan. Then in verse four, a great sword with death, then the fourth seal with death so that one fourth of all men will die. Now by my rough calculations, that's one and a half billion people.

Carl Sagan is worried, not about AIDS, not about the situation in the Persian Gulf, but about some cloud that will puff up, shield the sun, and cause, by his calculations, a billion people to die. Carl Sagan, read Revelation 6.

Revelation 6:9, the fifth seal is broken, and murders break out. Revelation 6:12, the sixth seal: There will be a great earthquake, the sun will be blackened, the moon will turn to blood, the stars will fall, more earthquakes, and men will look for places to hide and find no relief.

Now in Revelation 8:1, as the seventh seal is opened, there was quietness for half an hour. It's like saying, "Pause, and notice what God is doing to get your attention." And then the trumpets. Now trumpets can announce worship and celebration or war and judgment. These seven announce war and judgment. Revelation 8:7: There will be great hail, fire, and bloodshed. It will be so great that a third of all the trees will be destroyed. It could be that some nuclear weapons are involved here. Revelation 8:8: The second trumpet, and a third of all the seas turn to blood, and a third of all the life in the sea will die. A third of all the ships will be destroyed. Would it be reading too much between the lines to say that there will be a sea battle?

Revelation 8:10: With the third trumpet, all the waters will become poisoned, and many will die. In verse twelve, the fourth trumpet alters the sun, moon, and stars.

Revelation 9:1 says that out of the bottomless pit of Hell will come demons to inflict pain on men. Mom and Dad, look at your children. If you have any love for them, you should sit down with them and share the gospel. Tell them that with Christ there is hope, there's life, as opposed to going through this kind of judgment. Verse thirteen, with the sixth trumpet a huge army, out of the East, with two hundred million men will march with destruction upon the earth. In addition, Ezekiel says that amongst Russia and six other nations, five of them will die. Israel will be cut off.

Finally, in Revelation 12, it says there will be a war in Heaven. In chapter thirteen, everyone must take on the mark of the Beast, or there will be no food, no job, no hope. And then God gets mad. God says He will pour out His wrath. Now the wrath of God was poured out on Christ when He died on the cross. So if I accept Christ as my Savior, it means that the wrath of God was put on Christ on the cross, and God will never pour His wrath on anyone who accepts Christ.

After all the earth has endured, God will pour out His wrath. In chapter sixteen, painful sores will afflict people. The sea will be so filled with death it will begin to stink. The waters will turn to blood. Men will be scorched with fire and see major portions of the earth burnt up. Then darkness will come that will be painful. Unclean spirits will come, and this continues until the Bible says, "It's done."

You have a choice. You can either go to the cross where God says it's finished, where eternal life was finished and secured for you, or you can go to the Tribulation where God says it's done. For every soul that has come to that point and not received Christ, their opportunity to receive Christ is over. It's over forever.

Back in chapter seventeen, religion fails. Do you know that religion is the enemy of the cross? It's one of the calamities of Bible prophecy. The Bible says that in the last day evil spirits in the churches will be seducing men and women, telling them a false message, a false hope. Political system will fail. The economic systems will fail. And when all of that is done, Armageddon begins. The Persian Gulf War was like a lady finger firecracker compared to Armageddon. But I know God can use this war to bring people to God. Would you come today? The final calamity is that people won't come.

# *The Challenge Of Bible Prophecy*

Every day I pray that God will make me want to have a sensitivity toward people who want to be saved. The most critical thing in talking about the last days is to get people to see that salvation is available now, but it might not be available ten minutes from now.

Acts 16 describes a man with a political position, the keeper of the prison, an up and coming man. In a manner of speaking, he was ready to bring justice to Paul and Silas. God sent an earthquake to his little prison, shaking the earth, releasing the prisoners, and breaking the jail. Paul and Silas gathered the prisoners, keeping them there in the jail. When this man saw that these prisoners were not afraid of death or earthquakes or punishment, he brought them out. In verse 30, we read:

> *"And brought them out, and said, what must I do to be saved?"*

There is the challenge of Bible prophecy. The challenge of Bible prophecy is for people to see what is ahead, and then ask, "What must I do to be saved?" A teenager might have been raised in a home where the Bible was read and God was reverenced but where he never trusted Christ. Or an adult may have fooled people for years and have been very religious but still not be saved. Are you ready?

This man at the jail was probably a religious man. But when he saw God create just a little earthquake and shake his prison, he asked, "What must I do to be saved?" Now, if he had gone to some people today, they might have said, "Look, you don't want to be saved. You're just coming out of fright. You're worried unnecessarily." But this man had every reason to be worried. If a man isn't saved, he ought to worry. It's a time to worry. It's a time to ask how to be saved.

And the answer people give is: Join a good church, tithe regularly. No, that's a perversion. Keep the Ten Commandments? If you were to try to keep the Ten Commandments, most of you would break them in ten minutes.

I remember one time my dad said that when he got saved, he decided to keep the Ten Commandments. He couldn't do it. So one day I decided to keep the Ten Commandments. For three or four days, my mother only had to suggest something, and I did it. About the fourth day, my mother said to do something, and I said, "Aw, Mom. . . ." Hmmm. Broke that one. And the Bible says if you break one, you break them all.

So Paul doesn't say, "Join a church." He doesn't say, "Be baptized." There are more people going to Hell wet than any other way. I'm tired of people saying, "But you have to be baptized for salvation." No, my friend, if you had to be baptized to be saved, then what about the thief on the cross? He was guaranteed by God that he would be in Heaven. Why? Because he took the death of Christ on the cross as payment for his sin. Nothing could be clearer.

Am I against baptism? Absolutely not. But baptism is not salvation. It's the outward showing that we belong to Christ. We read in Acts 16:31:

*"And they said, Believe on the Lord Jesus Christ, and thou shalt be saved, and thy house."*

If his family would believe, they would also be saved. Isn't that great? Have you ever done that? The challenge of Bible prophecy is, has it affected you personally?

The other challenge is the Judgment Seat of Christ. This is for those who are saved. Those who know Christ and have received Him as Savior will be caught up to meet Him in the clouds according to 1 Thessalonians 4:16-17. At that moment, any doubt that you've had about the worth and value of Christ will be gone. You'll see Him in all His beauty. Will you wish you had lived your life differently? You can live it differently right now.

The Bible says that God will examine the way we have lived our lives. Based on how we lived, God will reward us. For those who have not lived their lives for Him, and have disappointed Him time and time again, they will first of all be forgiven. I thrill in that, don't you? If we confess our sins, He is just and able to forgive our sins. They're gone. What about those who confess their sins but then do nothing? The Bible says they will receive no reward. The tragedy will be seeing Christ in all His glory and all His beauty and then having nothing to give back to Him. We might wish we could go back and live life differently, but it will be too late.

Later today, Christ may come. If you're not ready, in terms of salvation, it will be too late. If you're not ready in terms of having your life committed to Him, it will be too late. What can you do?

In Philippians 4:1, believers are called "my joy and crown." Did you know that there is a crown for those who win others to Christ? You might think you can't talk with others. Then you can pray. I'm convinced there's a soul winner's crown for those who pray for the salvation of others. You can pray.

There is a crown for those who live a holy life, for those who put their thoughts and actions in subjection to Christ. There is a crown for those who love His appearing. That's the one I want. I want to love His appearing. I want to be a fanatic. I want to be known as ridiculous because I actually think Christ may come. That's the challenge of living today.

If God said it, if God wrote it, it's going to happen. That's the certainty of Bible prophecy. And the calamity of Bible prophecy is to have the invitation and turn it down. The challenge is to ask, "Has it ever affected me?"

Do you know Christ as your Savior? According to the Bible, there is no hope apart from the finished work of Jesus Christ on the cross. I pray that God will do a work in your heart and your life. As we have watched the war in Iraq, thirty or forty points of Bible prophecy have been exactly fulfilled as they were written by a Bible prophet twenty-five hundred years ago. You know, Jean Dixon didn't even predict the war, let alone a single detail.

Will you accept the challenge and let it affect your life? I'd like you to come to Jesus Christ. Would you do it? You can know that if the trumpet were to sound today, you'd be ready. Are you ready? Are you living for Christ? Don't be caught in the calamity when you can know the Christ of the Bible as your Savior in certainty. Answer the challenge. Come to Christ now.